The Little Angel

The Bridge Between Two Worlds

Written & Illustrated

by Leia A. Stinnett

ISBN 0-929385-85-3

Published by

StarChild Press
a division of
Light Technology
Publishing
P.O. Box 1526
Sedona, Arizona 86339
(520) 282-6523

Printed by

**MISSION
POSSIBLE
Commercial
Printing**

P.O. Box 1495
Sedona, AZ 86339

The Bridge Between Two Worlds

9.8.09

Sarah stood out on her back steps her head turned upward, almost perpendicular to the ground. Staring up at the deep night sky, her large, dark brown eyes were filled with awe as she scanned the millions of twinkling lights as though she were looking for something very important.

Out of the myriad of stars dotting the sky, there was one single star Sarah searched for night after night — one star that seemed to draw her into its magnificence.

Toward this one particular star, she felt a very special connection — a warmth, a strong bond, a feeling of belonging. These feelings were very difficult for her to explain to others. Sarah wasn't sure

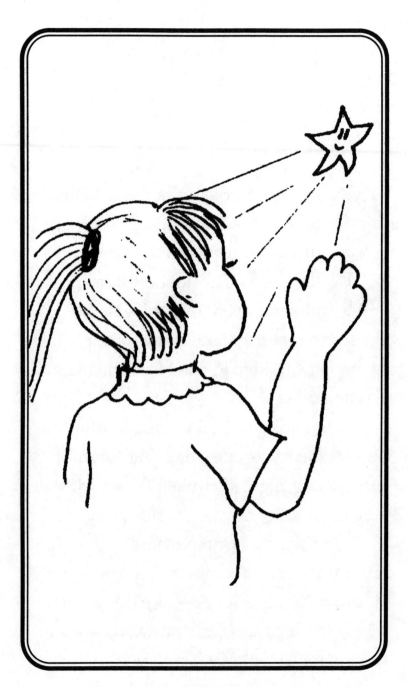

about these feelings herself.

Yes, there it was. Her special little diamond in the sky.

There was one very large, bright star that seemed to twinkle colors of red, blue, green and silver. Sarah watched the light show intently, rarely blinking her eyes for fear of losing sight of this very special place.

Tonight as Sarah gazed at this beautiful star tears welled up in her eyes and soon, trickled down her cheeks. Inside her heart was a longing to go *home* — wherever home was. She didn't understand this feeling. After all, wasn't Earth her home?

Didn't she have a family who loved her?

Didn't she have lots of nice things, just about everything a girl her age could wish for?

But deep inside, she realized she was unhappy. She was different than her

parents and her two brothers. In fact, Sarah often wondered if she had been adopted. She would even try many, many times to ask her parents about her adoption, but the words stuck in her throat.

Sarah had written a very special poem to her star. The poem just seemed to flow from her pen one night as she watched the star from her bedroom window. Tonight, she added a rather alluring tune to the words:

"Twinkle, twinkle, star so bright,
As I watch you through the night,
I see a face looking down at me,
I wonder just who
This face could be.
Even though you're so far above,
I can still feel
Your very special love.
And when I feel so all alone,
I look up at you and feel safe —
I'm home!"

As Sarah sang her special song to her beautiful star, the flashing colors seemed to draw her into a special place deep within herself, a special place where she let her thoughts take her back to the time when she was born.

She could remember a great deal about her life as an infant from discussions she heard between her parents and their friends. There were times when Sarah would actually see images or pictures of herself as a baby and small child. She always felt as though she was actually there, reliving a part of her growing-up years.

She remembered her mother telling friends about Sarah's difficult birth. "It was as though she did not want to be born," Sarah's Mom would say.

She also remembered crying a lot as a baby, rarely sleeping more than an hour or two through the night. She had visions of her worn-out parents holding her, rocking

her, trying every way they could think of to get her to close her eyes and sleep.

Sarah felt unhappy even as a tiny infant, but unhappy about what?

She was very sensitive to her environment. Her parents were forced to move to a drier climate because of her chronic sinus problems and headaches. She had some relief in their new home, but the problem was always there.

Bright light hurt Sarah's eyes. She had to cover her eyes with sunglasses or with her hands when she went outdoors.

She had the ability to hear even the slightest of sounds – sounds other people could not even hear.

In fact, all of her senses were very keen, particularly her ability to feel what other people were feeling.

Many times she would walk up to total strangers, touch their shoulder and tell them everything was okay, that God loved

them and she loved them so they should not feel so bad.

When Sarah felt someone around her was sad, she was sad, even to the point of having tears form in her eyes. She felt other people's joy, love, anger and grief. Sarah was aware of feelings everywhere, and this was not always an enjoyable experience for her.

Because of her ability to feels people's emotions, Sarah was especially fond of being outside by herself, enjoying God's beautiful world. She loved the trees, especially the old willow tree in her backyard. This tree told her stories of long ago about all the people who had come to sit under its long, wispy branches.

This tree helped her feel safe. She could tuck herself up against the sturdy trunk and disappear from the world, hidden in the graceful branches of the old willow tree. She would sing as the branches moved to and fro in the gentle breeze.

Sarah loved the flowers. She would play a game with them, imagining each flower was a beautiful little person with its own feelings and thoughts and its own personal name.

She often sang to the flowers — a beautiful song about a faraway place in the stars. She was never sure where the words or tune had come from, but it was a song that made her feel safe.

She collected different rocks, lined them up on her windowsill and on top of her dresser.

Each rock seemed to come alive when Sarah was present. Sarah talked to them, treating them like very special friends.

All the rocks were special — from the most beautiful crystal to the most plain, gray rock with the funny shape. Sarah felt each one was important. They each had something special to do or, she figured, they would not be here on Earth at all.

She would keep them a while and then return them to the places she had found them, tucking them neatly and securely into the earth. Sarah felt they could best do their work if the rocks were where God had placed them in the first place. She could borrow them, but she did not feel right about keeping them from their place in the yard.

She would sit for hours in the trees behind her house and play with the many birds and animals that would wander in close enough for her to talk to. She had a special way she communicated with them — she would think up something in her mind, and the birds and animals seemed to know exactly what she had thought. They responded in various ways to her thoughts — moving closer to her, turning their heads, flapping their wings, blinking their eyes. Sarah always knew when the animals were talking back to her.

16

It was not uncommon to see wild birds sitting on Sarah's shoulders, and the deer, raccoons, porcupines and other wild animals resting at her feet or sharing in the special lunches Sarah would prepare for all her friends.

Sarah had a great imagination. She would lie in the tall grass and stare up at the soft, fluffy clouds moving gently with the breeze. She would imagine herself living in another time in history, in another country. She saw herself as an Egyptian priestess, covered with gold and jewels, wearing a beautiful white gown with a gold and purple satinlike robe.

She imagined herself as a Native American warrior, bow and arrows in hand, riding a beautiful white horse across the mountains, the wind moving like flowing water through long, thick, black hair.

Sarah saw herself as a minister standing in front of a large group of people,

telling them how much God loved them —
all the people in the universe.

Sarah also saw herself in a very
different body — it made her laugh. She
saw herself with long, silvery arms and legs
and large, almond-shaped eyes. She did
not understand what this image was all
about, but it was fun. It was different —
different like she was.

For a moment, her thoughts brought
her back to the reality of her gazing at the
glittering star. Then, just as quickly, her
imagination took her back to the time
when she was only five years old — back to
the secret meeting, the meeting she had
told no one about.

Late one night when her parents were
sound asleep, Sarah was awakened by a loud
buzzing sound in her right ear. She saw a
flash of brilliant white light in her mind's
eye. She didn't understand how she could
see this light when her eyes were closed, but

it seemed unimportant next to the event that followed the flashing light.

Sarah opened her eyes. Next to her bed was á figure surrounded in white and gold light, a light one would think too bright to look at without hurting one's eyes, yet she found the light loving and gentle. The light seemed familiar to Sarah. She was not afraid.

The figure stepped forward. Long, golden hair framed the face of a beautiful woman dressed in a silvery blue gown. There was a radiance about her — a radiance of total love and compassion. Sarah felt comfortable and very excited.

As the woman began to speak Sarah noticed her golden wings and a beautiful golden light radiating from her, filling the entire room.

"I have come to tell you, Sarah, you are very special. You have much to share with the world when you grow up. Know

that God loves you, and whenever you feel lonely or sad, call my name — Sonya — I will be with you always."

The message was brief but comforting to the small child. With those words, Sonya disappeared into the night.

At age five, Sarah did not really understand what had happened, nor who this beautiful person was.

As she grew older, she realized she had been visited by an angel of God, her guardian angel. She always felt better when she called upon Sonya to be with her. Sonya always made her feel safe.

Sarah's life was a very lonely one. She did not make friends easily. She was very quiet and oftentimes stayed off by herself, rather than getting involved in the games of other children.

She did not feel she belonged in this world. She felt different. She did not want to do what the older children wanted to do

9.17.09

24

and, because of this, they began to ignore her more and more.

Sarah preferred to do quiet things by herself such as drawing, writing and reading books about other worlds. Sometimes she would be so absorbed in her reading that the teacher would have to come looking for her to remind her to return to the classroom after lunch or recess.

Sarah was born with some very special gifts — gifts all people have, but gifts that for some are very developed.

Sarah did not fully understand how to use these special talents, and they were not something she could easily discuss with her family and others.

As a small child, she had many strange experiences that became her little secrets. As she grew older, she wasn't sure they were anymore than a small child's imagination.

But as she grew older, her special gifts

became more and more prevalent in her life — stronger, more clear.

One of Sarah's great gifts was her ability to know what other people were thinking, what they were going to say before they said anything. Some people thought this very odd; others were a bit afraid of Sarah.

Sarah could feel things and know things were going to happen several hours, days or even weeks before the event actually took place. Other times she would dream of the event, and the event would take place just as she had dreamt it.

Sarah could see pictures in her mind's eye. Every now and then, when she was resting on her bed, eyes closed, she would see colors. Usually she saw purple and green and every now and then a flash of white light.

She really did not know what these colors meant, but she felt they were very

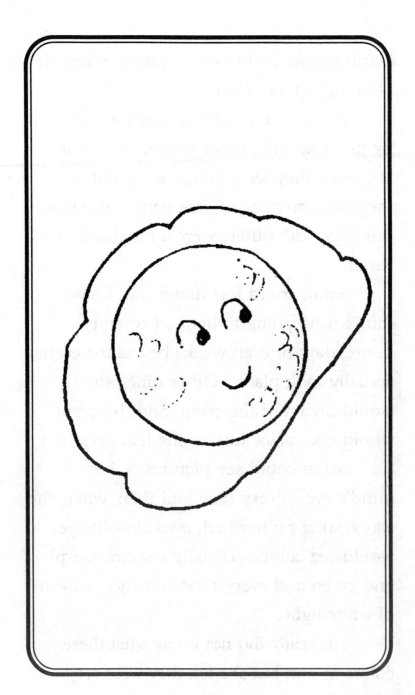

beautiful. As the colors swirled together, she felt a comforting, healing sensation throughout her body.

She could see colored lights flitting about her bedroom. She could see tiny fairies in the garden around beautiful flowers. Every now and then, Sarah could see Sonya watching over her, sending her love and warm thoughts.

There was one picture that appeared quite regularly now in Sarah's mind — a picture of something that looked like a planet or a star far out in space. She didn't recognize it as being one of the planets in our solar system, and she searched through every science book she could get her hands on looking for a place that looked like this planet in her visions.

The planet appeared to be purple in color — unlike anything she had ever seen before. When she saw the planet in her vision, she felt peace and serenity. The

planet seemed to be tucked safely away in some secret corner of God's wondrous universe, far away.

Sarah did not realize at this time, however, that very soon this planet would play an important role in her life.

She discovered another special gift while on the playground one day at school. One of her schoolmates had a terrible headache. Sarah could feel the pain in her own head, but she resisted what she felt an urging to do.

When the impulse became so great that she could no longer resist, she walked over to Christy and placed her hands on Christy's head.

In a few moments, Christy jumped up with a startled look in her eyes and a half-smile on her face.

"Sarah, what did you do? My headache is all gone . . . like magic! What did you do?" asked a very grateful, but

startled Christy.

"I . . . I don't know," said Sarah, her voice carrying a puzzled tone. "I'm not sure. I just felt your head needed a little love, so I touched it with my hands and thought about how much God loves us all. I asked God to send a whole bunch of love into your head and help you feel better!"

Christy was very confused. On one hand, she was overjoyed that Sarah had "fixed" her headache. On the other hand, Christy was afraid of Sarah, wondering what kind of magical powers she had and in what other ways Sarah might be able to use them.

Sarah did have one best friend, her Aunt Lisa.

Aunt Lisa lived alone in a very large, older home in walking distance from Sarah's house.

Sarah wished over and over that she could live with Aunt Lisa. Aunt Lisa told

Sarah her parents would miss her very much, and they loved her and wanted her to live with them. However, Aunt Lisa did tell her many, many times, "You can visit me any time you want, Sarah. I love you very much. I am here to help you."

Aunt Lisa's hair was silver. She wore it tied up in a bun on top of her head. She was a tall slender woman with dark, compelling eyes. Aunt Lisa looked about half of her 75 years, and she reminded Sarah of a character she had read about in one of her favorite science fiction novels.

Aunt Lisa would take Sarah for walks and together they would talk to the animals, plants and trees . . . even the tiny insects.

Aunt Lisa taught Sarah how to communicate with all the things in nature. "Yes Sarah, plants, trees, rocks and all of the animals can truly tell what we are saying to them," Aunt Lisa assured Sarah.

Together they practiced games, testing their memory and their ability to see things with their eyes closed. Aunt Lisa had made up a very special game for Sarah. She would hide an object somewhere in her house and then ask Sarah to find it by feeling the energy. This was a very frustrating game for a while, but soon, Sarah became very adept at finding the items Aunt Lisa hid from her.

Aunt Lisa helped Sarah with her studies. Then, they would have lessons of their own. Aunt Lisa would tell Sarah about how much God loved all of the Earth and all of the people of Earth, but how He/She wished everyone was more loving and kind toward each other.

Together they thought of ways they could help people understand how God truly felt and how each person on Earth could help create for themselves and others a happier, healthier, more joyful and

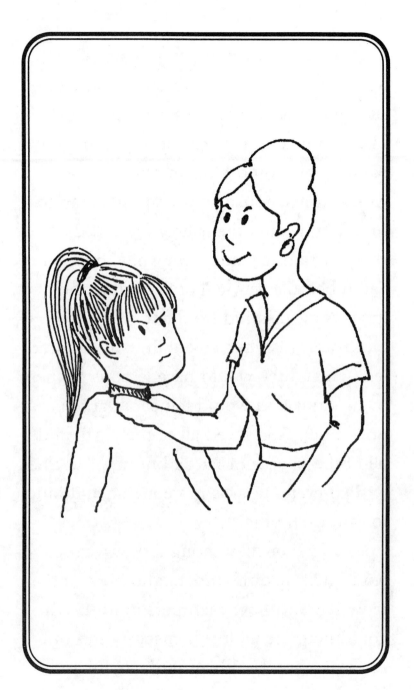

38

loving place to live.

One day in particular Sarah was feeling very depressed and lonely. She left school and walked straight to Aunt Lisa's house. Tears filled her eyes as she knocked on Aunt Lisa's door.

"Why Sarah, what's wrong?" asked Aunt Lisa.

"Oh Aunt Lisa, I don't know. I don't belong here. I keep having this vision of a faraway place, a
purple planet, far out in the
universe. I don't know why, but it feels like my *real* home.

"I keep feeling unhappy. I feel what everyone else is feeling — good or bad. It makes me unhappy to see everyone else so sad or angry at each other. It makes me sad that people want to make wars. They want to destroy the beautiful Earth and all of her creatures."

"Oh Sarah, I know how you feel.

9.29.09

40

Come, let me share some special things with you." Aunt Lisa led Sarah to her meditation room — a room decorated in beautiful white, gold and purple satin pillows and colorful shear curtains.

A white candle was set up on an altar. A picture of Jesus was hanging on the wall behind the candle, looking at Sarah with compassion in His eyes.

Two very large crystals lay on the altar in front of the candle — What peace, what beauty, thought Sarah as she began to quiet down.

"I was very different, too. When I was your age, I didn't want to be here. I thought I was adopted. I thought no one on this Earth loved or wanted me.

"Then I started seeing colored lights, angels and beings from other planets, but I didn't know why. There was no one I could tell my experience to, no one I felt would understand.

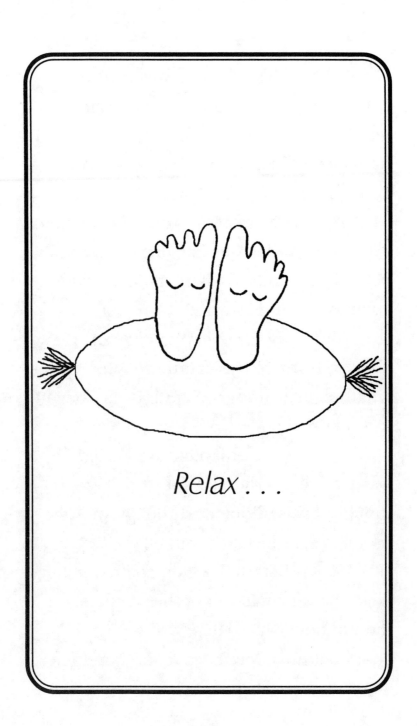

Relax . . .

"I could read people's minds . . ."

"I can do that," interrupted Sarah.

"I know," responded Aunt Lisa, without even losing her train of thought.

"I talked to invisible people, and I still do. I talk to the angels I see now. I talk to the people from other planets, the extraterrestrials. You see, my *real* home is not this Earth — nor is Earth *your* true home!"

"I don't understand," said Sarah, with a frown on her face telling Aunt Lisa she did not understand what Aunt Lisa was saying.

"Come Sarah, I will take you on a journey to your true home. I will ask God to protect you in His/Her loving light. I will ask your guardian angel to accompany you as I take you on a very special journey to another world.

"Come Sarah, close your eyes. Lie back on the nice, soft cushions, close your eyes, breathe deeply and let your imagination take you on a special journey.

*Close your eyes. Breathe deeply —
inhale as you count to eight and exhale as
you count to eight.*

*Breathe in and out until you begin to
feel calm and relaxed in your body.*

*Now, let your toes relax. Bring the
relaxing energy into your feet, your heels and
ankles. Let your feet relax completely.*

*Now, let your legs relax. Start with the
calves of your legs, then relax your knees and
your thighs. Bring the relaxing energy up into
the base of your spine, up into your hips and
around the front of your body to the abdomen.*

*Let the relaxing energy move into your
stomach and on up into your chest. Then
move the relaxing energy all the way up to the
top of your shoulders.*

*Now let the relaxing energy move from
the top of your shoulders down through your
upper arms, past your elbows, into your forearms and into your wrists, hands, fingers and
thumbs.*

Let your arms, hands and fingers relax.

Then bring your relaxing energy back up from your fingers and thumbs through your forearms, elbows and upper arms. Let the relaxing energy move up into your neck and let your neck relax completely.

Move the relaxing energy on up into your face, your jaw and your head . . . all the way to the top of your head. Let your whole body relax completely.

Now, focus on the spot in the back of your eyes. Imagine a beautiful blue light. Let this light grow larger and larger until all you can see is the blue light. Then breathe, relax andconcentrate on the blue light while I take you on a very special journey into the universe to another world, a beautiful world of light.

Let your mind travel back in time, back to a time before you ever came to live on planet Earth. All the way back. Let your mind travel. Know you are safe and protected in God's love and light as you travel back in time.

*See yourself traveling through space.
You can imagine you are in a special kind of
spacecraft, one in which there are no controls.
You are simply moving through space – past
the stars, the Moon and other planets. You
can see all these beautiful bodies in space as
you travel into the universe.*

*At a distance you can see what looks
like another world. It is a tiny round spot.
As you move in closer, the spot grows quickly to a large planet that appears orange and
green and white in color.*

*Suddenly you find yourself flying above
the ground. You move swiftly through a purple archway, what looks like a special bridge.
You can see a beautiful purple landscape.*

*At a distance you can see purple
mountains and a lavender sky. Beautiful
colors radiate from a crystal city, perched
high on a purple cliff to your right. Now,
you move in closer and closer.*

Soon you can see this crystal city in all

48

its splendor. It is truly the most magnificent city you have ever seen. It twinkles like a million stars, and you can feel love, peace, joy and harmony.

In the center of this city, in what looks like a huge park full of crystals, flowers and golden temples, you can see many different types of buildings. Some are shaped like domes, or circles. Some are like pyramids. Some are pyramids with circles on top . . . all different shapes.

You are greeted by a crowd of beings. These beings do not have bodies like we do on Earth. These beings are true light. They are happy to see you. These are your true friends and family. This is what you looked like before you took on an Earth body.

You can feel the love from the hearts of these beings. They truly love you. They know you have come to Earth to help humankind learn about God and to become one people, unified in love and sharing. They tell you they support you in your work. They are very proud you have chosen to help God in this way.

They tell you your name – your star name – Alia Za-Á. You feel wonderful. You know you are home!

You sit together, you and your star family – your true family. They tell you how you chose to do some important work for God. They tell you how you chose to come to Earth and help people find their pathway back to God, the Creator.

They tell you that many people of Earth lost their way, getting caught up in a world of material things – money, fancy houses, cars, clothes and the like. People began to feel these things were more important than loving each other and loving God.

So little star child, you have chosen, with thousands of other star children just like you, to come to Earth from this faraway star of beauty and love, to give unselfishly of yourself to help God's great Earth.

Your job is to teach people about God — how to find God deep within themselves, how to heal themselves, how to create a world of love, unity and
perfection. This is your purpose.

Your job is not an easy one, but it is a very important one. You have a lot of love and support from those of us here, from all the angels and heavenly beings in God's great universe.

As you grow up, more and more of your true being will return to your memory. You shall do great work for your Father/Mother.

You have come from a place of love and joy. Thus, it is very easy for you to teach others about these feelings.

Sometimes it is very painful on Earth because you don't receive love and compassion from people on Earth. But know that if you continue to send out love to all people, you will receive much more love in return.

51

Everything balances out in God's universe.

Every time you feel unhappy, every time you long for home, think of us. Remember how important you are to the Earth and her people, to all her
living things. Remember, you will play an important role in helping bring peace to Earth and good will among all people of all nations.

Now, let your mind return to the blue light in the center of your forehead. Breathe deeply and let your mind become aware of the room around you.

"Open your eyes and be in the present moment."

In a flash, Sarah was back from her journey. There were tears of
happiness and joy in her eyes.

"Oh Aunt Lisa, I went to this beautiful place. I saw these beautiful people . . . or beings . . . my family. Did I really see home? Is this the place I find in the sky

each night — my special star?" asked
Sarah.

"Yes, Sarah, it is!" said Aunt Lisa. "It
is your true home.

"You chose to come to Earth from this
beautiful star so far away. Humankind on
Earth had forgotten about God. When God
asked for
volunteers, very special people from many
distant stars and planets responded with
love and willingly descended to Earth to
help people find the peace and love of God
deep within their hearts.

"When you chose to come to Earth,
you chose also to be born into an Earth
body. You can see from your meditation
that on your special star you were in quite a
different body.

"You chose to live on Earth in an Earth
body so you could help people without
frightening them. But you and I know,
even with an Earth body, we are different.

"We have special gifts of healing and intuition — knowing things before they happen, feeling things, whether comfortable or not. We are here to teach people about God. We are here to teach people how to heal themselves, how to create a perfect world of love and beauty and joy.

"You are a child of God, a child of the stars, a very aware little girl, wise beyond your thirteen years. You have lived on Earth but a few times, just to learn the experiences you will need to complete your task.

"You, Sarah, are a bridge between two worlds. You live in this world, but you are not a part of it. You are here to help people understand that there is life on other planets, that we are all living aspects of God — living, learning, loving and sharing.

"Sarah, you are a child of the stars. I, too, yearn to go home to my real home, but for now I am happy right where I am here on Earth.

"I have you to love and share with. I am here to learn things I could not learn on my home planet. I have found great satisfaction in helping those people I have taught here on Earth.

"Earth is your home, too. Star child, let your heart shine, filled with the radiance of God. Let your heart be filled with God's love, and let that love pour out upon this planet, into the hearts of every person.

"You will see, Sarah. Love will change this Earth into a beautiful place where all people will exist together as one people. All people will share and help one another. All people will respect the Earth and her living creatures.

"Then Sarah, with your job well done, you can go home!"

Heart Lights

Where I go, not all can follow,
But I walk a path that all can see.
It takes one moment to remember,
That children of God, of love, are we.
I beckon you to come in love,
To come in light and peace,
To cleanse yourselves
of life's emotions,
Let all the turmoil cease.
And be the angels that you are,
Loving, laughing, playing . . . free!
God placed a crystal in our hearts,
For us to shine, for all to see.
Like a diamond in the deep night sky,
Our heart light shines above,
For we shall never be alone, you see,
We have each other's love . . .

From another star child,
Ariel Aleah Za-Á

Other Books by Leia Stinnett:

A Circle of Angels
The Twelve Universal Laws

The Little Angel Books Series:
The Angel Told Me to Tell You Good-bye
Color Me One
Crystals R for Kids
Exploring the Chakras
Happy Feet
One Red Rose
When the Earth Was New
Where is God?
Who's Afraid of the Dark?

All My Angel Friends (Coloring Book)

About the Author

The '80s were a decade of self-discovery for Leia Stinnett after she began researching many different avenues of spirituality. In her profession as a graphic designer she had become restless, knowing there was something important she had to do outside the materiality of corporate America.

In August 1986 Leia had her first contact with Archangel Michael when he appeared in a physical form of glowing blue light. A voice said, "I am Michael. Together we will save the children."

In 1988 she was inspired by Michael to teach spiritual classes in Sacramento, California, the Circle of Angels. Through these classes she had the opportunity to work with learning-disabled children, children of abuse and those from dysfunctional homes.

Later Michael told her, "Together we are going to write the Little Angel Books." To date Leia and Michael have created thirteen Little Angel Books that present various topics of spiritual truths and principles. The books proved popular among adults as well as children.

The Circle of Angels classes have been introduced to several countries around the world and across the U.S., and Leia and her husband Douglas now have a teacher's manual and training program for people who wish to offer spiritual classes to children. Leia and Michael have been interviewed on Canadian Satellite TV and have appeared on NBC-TV's *Angels II – Beyond the Light,* which featured their Circle of Angels class and discussed their books and Michael's visit.

The angels have given Leia and Douglas a vision of a new educational system without competition or grades — one that supports love and positive self-esteem, honoring all children as the independent lights they are. Thus they are now writing a curriculum for the new "schools of light" and developing additional books and programs for children.